D0672491

MINI CLASSICS
BRER RABBIT
AND THE
BRAMBLE PATCH
And Other Stories

RETOLD BY STEPHANIE LASLETT
ILLUSTRATED BY STEPHEN HOLMES

‖ •PARRAGON• ‖

TITLES IN SERIES I AND III OF THE MINI CLASSICS INCLUDE:

FOR LIZ

A PARRAGON BOOK

Published by
Parragon Books,
Unit 13–17, Avonbridge Trading Estate,
Atlantic Road, Avonmouth, Bristol BS11 9QD

Produced by
The Templar Company plc,
Pippbrook Mill, London Road, Dorking, Surrey RH4 1JE

Designed by Mark Kingsley-Monks

Printed and bound in Great Britain

ISBN 1-85813-778-0

Many years ago on a cotton plantation down in the deep south of North America there lived an old black slave called Uncle Remus. Every evening as the sun set behind the persimmon trees and the shadows lengthened across the dusty yard, Uncle Remus would sit in his creaky old rocking chair on the cool

verandah, light his pipe and
tell his tales to anyone who
would care to listen. The
children sat with eyes as
round as saucers, and if they
were good and quiet then
they could listen too, and so
they heard all about the days
when animals strolled around
just the same as us folks.

These are some of those
stories that Uncle Remus
told long ago.

Brer Fox was having a hard think. He was fed up with that no-good Brer Rabbit strutting about telling the world what a darned clever Rabbit he was. Brer Fox knew he had twice the brains that Rabbit would *ever* have, even if he waited a month of Sundays. He would teach that boastful creature a thing or too. Yes, sirree, he would teach that Rabbit a lesson he would not forget!

After a while a big smile lit up his face and he went to work. He fetched some black tar and mixed it with turpentine and made himself the strangest little doll you ever did see, and he called that doll his Tar Baby! He put a straw hat on top of her head and very carefully he

picked her up and sat her
down right plumb in the
middle of the road. Then he
hid himself in the bushes to
see what would happen next.

Well, he didn't have long
to wait for who should come
sauntering down the road,
lippity-clippity, clippity-
lippity, but that Brer Rabbit
just as sassy as a jaybird. Brer
Fox, he lay low. Brer Rabbit
came closer and closer,
looking as if he owned the
whole world. Then he caught
sight of the Tar Baby and
boy, what a surprise he got!

Up he reared on his hind legs and his jaw dropped open. What in tarnation was this? The Tar Baby sat still and Brer Fox, he lay low.

"Mornin'!" says Brer Rabbit, tipping his hat politely. "Nice weather this mornin'," says he.

But that Tar Baby says nothing, and Brer Fox, he lay low. "And how are you this fine mornin'?" says

Brer Rabbit. That Tar Baby till says nothing, and Brer Fox, he lay low. "What's the matter? You deaf or sumpin'?" says Brer Rabbit. "'Cos if you is, I can holler louder!" Tar Baby says nothing, and Brer Fox, he lay low.

Well, Brer Rabbit keeps on asking her questions and Tar Baby keeps on saying nothing and that Brer Fox, he just lay low.

"I reckon you're stuck up, that's what I reckon," says Brer Rabbit, getting mad. "I'm gonna teach you some manners," says he. "If you don't take off that hat and wish me howdy, I'm gonna bust your nose!"

Tar Baby says nothing and Brer Fox still lay low, but by now he has a pain in his stomach and an ache in his jaw from trying not to laugh!

Then Brer Rabbit pulls
back his paw and blip! he
swipes that Tar Baby right
on the side of her head!

Well, that was his first big
mistake for now he was well
and truly stuck! Try as he
might he could not pull free.

"If you don't let me go I'm gonna swipe you once more," cries Brer Rabbit, but Tar Baby, she says nothing and Brer Fox, he lay low. So blip! there was his other paw stuck fast. That poor Rabbit started yelling and shouting and soon he had both his hind legs fixed firmly on the sticky Tar Baby. Well, the tears just rolled down Brer Fox's cheeks, and would you believe it but Brer Rabbit only goes and butts that Tar Baby so now his head is stuck fast, too!

Then Brer Fox strolled from the bushes looking just as cool as a cucumber.

"Howdy, Brer Rabbit," says he. "You look kinda stuck up this mornin'!" and then he laughed till his sides ached. "Well, I reckon I got you this time," says Brer

Fox. "You've been struttin'
'round this neighbourhood
like you own the place,
puttin' on your fancy airs
and graces. Jus' who do you
think you is? Nobody asked
you to come and get so
friendly with this Tar Baby.
No, you jus' come along
and makes yourself all
familiar and sticks yourself
all over her, without so
much as an if you please."

"Well, you jus' wait there while I goes and lights myself a nice little fire ready for my Brer Rabbit barbecue!"

Now that Brer Rabbit was just as cunning as a barrel-load of crafty monkeys so he thought hard.

"Well, if I've gotta go, I've gotta go and I must say, I'd rather die basted in a good barbecue sauce than be thrown into that bramble patch. Jus' don't throw me in that there bramble patch, Brer Fox!" begged the wily Rabbit.

27

Brer Fox was surprised to hear this. He had expected Brer Rabbit to be terrified at the thought of being cooked on a fire.

"Well, I guess it's too much trouble to light a fire. Reckon I'm gonna hang you instead," he declared.

"You hang me jus' as high as you like, but please don't fling me in that briar patch!" pleaded Brer Rabbit.

29

"Shucks, ain't got no string," said Brer Fox. "Guess I'll have to drown you."

"Drown me jus' as deep as you please," cried Brer Fox, "but don't throw me in that there briar patch!"

"No water near here," said Brer Fox. "Ain't nothing for it but to skin you."

"Yes, skin me!" agreed Brer Rabbit. "Scratch out my eyeballs, tear out my hair, o jus' what you like but, please, please don't throw me in that briar patch!"

Well Brer Fox wanted to hurt Brer Rabbit just as bad as he could so he picked up that Rabbit by his hind legs and swung him once around his head and then chucked him straight into the briar patch! Then he dusted off his hands and waited for the howls of pain. But no howls came.

Just when he thought Brer
Rabbit must be good and
dead for sure, Brer Fox heard
someone calling his name.
There was Brer Rabbit sat
up on the hill, combing a
small speck of tar from his
ear, just as bold as you like!
Then Brer Fox realised he
had been well and truly
tricked and he seethed as the
Rabbit's voice floated down
to him.

"I was born and raised in that briar patch, Brer Fox. Born and raised in that briar patch!"

One day Brer Rabbit, Brer Fox, Brer Raccoon, Brer Bear and a whole lot of other critters were clearing a new patch of ground.

They had to prepare the land because they wanted to plant a fine crop of corn. It was a hot day, the sun blazed out of a cloudless sky and poor Brer Rabbit soon got tired of working in the fearsome heat.

He didn't let on to the others that he was tired because he knew they would call him lazy — and he didn't want that at all!

So he carried on pulling up the weeds and carrying off the thorn bushes until bye and bye he let out a loud yell.

"Oo, oo! I got a sharp thorn in my paw!" he cried, pretending to be in pain. Then he slipped off mighty quick to look for a good cool place to rest. After a while he came across a well with a bucket hanging down into its shady depths.

"That sure looks cool," says Brer Rabbit. "That looks the very place for me," and straightaway he hops into the bucket. Well, the bucket didn't stay still. No, sirree. That bucket dropped like a stone to the bottom of the well. Well, there hasn't ever been a beast quite so scared as poor Brer Rabbit was at that moment.

He knew where he had been a few seconds ago but now he had no idea where he was going! His stomach leapt right up from his belly and landed in his mouth and that ain't a nice place for it to be!

Suddenly the bucket hit the water, blam! Brer Rabbit hunched up good and tight and shivered. He hadn't been expecting this dreadful journey and he wasn't at all sure what might happen next.

Up above in the hot sunshine Brer Fox had stopped work. He always had one eye on what Brer Rabbit was up to and when he saw the rabbit sneak off from the clearing, he downed tools and set off after him. He guessed Brer Rabbit was up to no good but the only way to be sure was to sneak after him and watch. Brer Fox saw Brer Rabbit arrive at the well and stop. He saw him jump in the bucket. Then,

o and behold, he saw him
disappear out of sight.

Brer Fox was the most astonished
fox you ever set eyes on. He sat
in the bushes and thought and
thought but whichever way he
came at it he could make no
sense of it whatsoever.

"Well, if that ain't the darndest
thing I ever did see," he muttered
to himself. "There has to be a
mighty good reason why Brer
Rabbit has gone down that well."

Then he clapped his hand to his mouth. "Why, of course!" he cried. "Right down there in that well is where Brer Rabbit

keeps all his money hidden, and
if it ain't that, then he's gone and
discovered a gold mine, and if it
ain't that then I'm sure going to
find out just what it is!"

Slowly Brer Fox crept closer to the well and listened. There wasn't a single sound to be heard. Nearer and nearer he crept but still he heard nothing. He reached the well and slowly peered over the edge. Silence.

All this time poor Brer Rabbit was hunched up in that bucket, nearly scared out of his skin. He didn't dare so much as twitch a whisker for fear of the bucket tipping over and spilling him into the cold water. Suddenly a loud voice echoed down the well.

"Howdy, Brer Rabbit! Who are you visiting down there?" called Brer Fox.

"Me?" replied Brer Rabbit, suddenly as cool as a cucumber

Why, I'm just fishing, Brer Fox.
was up there working, getting
ind of hungry and I thought to
1yself, 'Why, reckon I'll just go
nd catch a few fine fish to
urprise my friends with for
inner' — and here I am, and
ere are the fishes."

Brer Fox licked his lips. "Are there many fish down there, Brer Rabbit?" says he.

"Many? *Many*? Are there many grains of sand on the seashore?" replied Brer Rabbit. "Why, this water is so chock full of fish it's almost alive." Brer Fox strained his eyes in the darkness to catch a sight of those wonderful fish.

"Come on down and help me haul them in, Brer Fox. I could do with a hand," said Brer Rabbit.

Brer Fox looked down into the dark shadows. He narrowed his eyes and looked doubtful.

"But how do I get down there, Brer Rabbit? It's awful deep down there," he said, with a shiver.

"Just jump in the bucket you see hanging from the bar, Brer Fox. It will bring you down safe and sound," replied Brer Rabbit, in as sweet and helpful a voice as could be.

Well, Brer Fox could not resist the thought of all those fishes jumping and leaping and his stomach sort of began to growl and pester him. So up he jumped into that bucket and down he went, down, down into the well. And sure enough, as he went down, the wily Brer Rabbit went up. The weight of the fox in the bucket was pulling the other bucket up to the top of the well.

As the two buckets passed one another half way down the well Brer Rabbit began to sing.

'Goodbye, Brer Fox,
take care of your clothes,
for this is the way the world goes.
Some goes up and some goes down,
you'll get to the bottom
all safe and sound.'

Soon the bucket hit the water
and Brer Rabbit reached the top
of the well. Out he jumped and
off he skedaddled back to the
clearing like a shot from a
soldier's musket.

"Hey, folks!" he cried. "That Brer Fox is in the well and muddying up our drinking water!"

The animals kicked up a ruckus like you've never heard and they were off to visit that well in no time.

Brer Rabbit ran on ahead and took great delight in yelling down the well.

'Here comes a man
with a great big gun.
When he hauls you up,
you jump and run!'

Then the animals hauled Brer Fox up out of the well and boxed his ears for dirtying the water. They wouldn't listen to explanations and excuses and pretty soon Brer Fox and Brer Rabbit were back at the clearing, working away as if they had never heard of a well, except that every now and then Brer Rabbit would burst out laughing and that old Brer Fox, he would look as mad, as mad could be.

65

Brer Fox wasn't much of a gardener; ask anybody, they'll all tell you the same thing. But one year he decided it was high time he got the hang of growing things for himself and he decided he would plant a peanut patch. Well, once he'd made his mind up to do it he was raring to go.

"I'm going to plant me some peanuts," he declared to the

world at large, and the words were hardly out of his mouth before the ground was freshly dug over and those peanut plants were firmly in place.

Over the other side of the fence sat Brer Rabbit. He watched all this hard work going on and every day he would sit there and sing softly to himself.

'Ti-yi! Tungalee!

I eat um pea, I pick um pea.

It grows in the ground,

it grows so free.

Ti-yi! good peanut pea!'

Sure enough, when those peanuts had grown big and ripe that Brer Rabbit, he helped himself just as sassy as you please. Every morning Brer Fox went down to his peanut patch all excited to inspect his crop and when he discovered that somebody had been scrabbling in and out of the plants he grew mighty mad.

He had his suspicions about
who the culprit might be but
that wily Brer Rabbit was careful
to cover up his tracks each day
and so Brer Fox was never able
to hunt him down.

One day Brer Fox was inspecting his beautiful peanut patch. He was mighty proud of that patch, and as cautious and protective as if each one of those plants was his own little child. He would never have believed the pleasure he got from raising those tender green shoots from seed. As he strolled by the fence that surrounded his garden he suddenly spied a small hole close to the ground.

"Blessed if that ain't where the little varmint who is stealing my peanuts gets through," he said to himself. Off he went to find some rope and, pulling a hickory sapling down to the ground, he tied that rope in a slip knot around the branch and pretty soon had made a darned good trap.

The next day ole Brer Rabbit came sashaying down the road and when he reached Brer Fox fence he bent down and wriggled through the hole. Sure enough, the rope slipped tight around his legs, the sapling flew up in the air and there hung Brer Rabbit, 'twixt heaven and earth! There he swung back and forth; one minute scared he was going to fall, the next minute scared he *wasn't* going to fall.

As he swung to and fro he tried to think up a tale to tell Brer Fox but before he had managed to come up with a story that he was perfectly satisfied with, who should he hear ambling down the road but Brer Bear.

"Howdy, Brer Bear!" cries Brer Rabbit. Brer Bear's huge head slowly turned from side to side. "Whassat? Whoosair?" he said. "I'm up here, Brer Bear," called Brer Rabbit.

"Look up in the hickory tree."
The big bear raised his head and
was astonished to see Brer
Rabbit hanging upside down,
just as calm and contented as
you like.

"Howdy, Brer Rabbit," he said. "And how are you this fine bee buzzing morning?"

"Fair to middling, Brer Bear," replies Brer Rabbit. "Fair to middling."

Brer Bear stood and stared.

"Brer Rabbit?" says Brer Bear, scratching his head. "Would yo mind telling me just what in th Sam Hill you is doing up in tha there tree?"

Brer Rabbit smiled down at

im in an upside down sort of
way and replied, "I'm earning a
dollar a minute, Brer Bear."
"A dollar a minute!" spluttered
Brer Bear. "That's pretty good
doing, Brer Rabbit."
"Sure is, and all I have to do is
keep the crows out of Brer Fox's
peanut patch."
Brer Rabbit looked at Brer Bear
and Brer Bear looked at Brer
Rabbit. After a while Brer Rabbit
spoke again.

"Say, I don't suppose you want the chance to earn a dollar a minute? I only ask because I know what a big family you have to feed what with all those children of yours. Gee, it must be mighty difficult to fill those little mouths."

Brer Bear nodded ruefully. "You never said a truer word, brother," he agreed. Then he looked up at the hickory tree. "Do you reckon I could do it?" he asked.

"Why, I reckon you was born to make a scarecrow," replied Brer Rabbit encouragingly, and soon he had told the bear exactly what to do. Brer Bear pulled down the sapling with one mighty paw and had soon freed Brer Rabbit from the rope.

Then placing both his huge feet back in the loop, he let go of the whippy tree and soon he was hanging upside down just exactly the same as Brer Rabbit had been two minutes earlier.

Brer Rabbit looked mighty happy to be down on the ground once again. He jumped twice in the air then skedaddle off to Brer Fox's house leaving Brer Bear swinging in the wind

"Brer Fox! Brer Fox!" cried ou

Brer Rabbit when he reached the porch. "Come on out and I'll show you the rascal who's been stealing your precious peanuts!"

Out bowled Brer Fox, stout walking stick in hand, and up the road they both ran, lickety-split.

"So that's your lowdown game, is it?" shouted Brer Fox when he caught sight of Brer Bear hanging in the wind. "You're the varmint who's been at my peanuts!"

Brer Bear had no time to explain that he was acting as a scarecrow to keep the birds off the peanut patch. Old Brer Fox didn't want to hear. He just set to with his stick and caught him a crack across his broad brown back.

"Oo! Ow!" wailed poor Brer Bear. "I was — ow! — looking after — oo! — your peanuts, Brer Fox!"

"Nibbling my best shoots!" BLAM! "Scrabbling up their little roots!" BLIM! "You call that looking after my plants?" BLAM! "You great loafer!" shouted Brer Fox as he worked hard with his stick. "Well, I'll know not to come to you when I need help with my gardening!" he cried.

Brer Rabbit nearly split his sides laughing but when he saw that Brer Fox had finished punishing Brer Bear and was cutting him free from the trap, he hightailed out of there for he was no fool, that rabbit.

He hid in a mud hole by the side of the road with just his eyes sticking out. Bye and bye Brer Bear came limping down the road. He spied these two round eyes and he stopped.

"Howdy, Brer Frog," he said. "You didn't happen to see Brer Rabbit coming down this way?"

"Knee-deep, knee-deep! He just went by a few minutes ago," replied that cunning Brer Rabbit in a croaky frog-like voice.

Brer Bear ground his teeth at the thought of how foolish he had been and off he lumbered down the road, muttering and moaning. And that Brer Rabbit jumped out of the mud hole, dried himself off in the sun, and sauntered off home to his family, same as any man.

JOEL CHANDLER HARRIS

The *Brer Rabbit* stories began as American
Negro fables, told by the slaves working on
plantations in the deep South of North America,
and almost certainly African in origin.
Joel Chandler Harris (1848-1908) insisted that
he did no more than simply retell the
stories, but in fact he showed great storytelling
skill in padding out what was often little more
than a folk saying. He also retained the
wonderfully rich dialect of the southern Negro
slaves, writing the words just as they would
have been said. This text has been adapted for
easier reading and understanding, but still
retains the flavour of Uncle Remus's relaxed
storytelling style.